The Talents run Mad; or, Eighteen Hundred and Sixteen. A satirical poem, in three dialogues with notes. By the author of "All the Talents" [E. S. Barrett].

Eaton Stannard Barrett

The Talents run Mad; or, Eighteen Hundred and Sixteen. A satirical poem, in three dialogues with notes ... By the author of "All the Talents" [E. S. Barrett].
Barrett, Eaton Stannard
British Library, Historical Print Editions
British Library
1816
8°.

The BiblioLife Network

This project was made possible in part by the BiblioLife Network (BLN), a project aimed at addressing some of the huge challenges facing book preservationists around the world. The BLN includes libraries, library networks, archives, subject matter experts, online communities and library service providers. We believe every book ever published should be available as a high-quality print reproduction; printed on- demand anywhere in the world. This insures the ongoing accessibility of the content and helps generate sustainable revenue for the libraries and organizations that work to preserve these important materials.

The following book is in the "public domain" and represents an authentic reproduction of the text as printed by the original publisher. While we have attempted to accurately maintain the integrity of the original work, there are sometimes problems with the original book or micro-film from which the books were digitized. This can result in minor errors in reproduction. Possible imperfections include missing and blurred pages, poor pictures, markings and other reproduction issues beyond our control. Because this work is culturally important, we have made it available as part of our commitment to protecting, preserving, and promoting the world's literature.

GUIDE TO FOLD-OUTS, MAPS and OVERSIZED IMAGES

In an online database, page images do not need to conform to the size restrictions found in a printed book. When converting these images back into a printed bound book, the page sizes are standardized in ways that maintain the detail of the original. For large images, such as fold-out maps, the original page image is split into two or more pages.

Guidelines used to determine the split of oversize pages:

• Some images are split vertically; large images require vertical and horizontal splits.
• For horizontal splits, the content is split left to right.
• For vertical splits, the content is split from top to bottom.
• For both vertical and horizontal splits, the image is processed from top left to bottom right.

THE TALENTS RUN MAD;

OR,

Eighteen Hundred and Sixteen.

A SATIRICAL POEM.

IN THREE DIALOGUES.

WITH NOTES.

BY

THE AUTHOR OF 'ALL THE TALENTS.'

AMABILIS INSANIA.

LONDON:
PRINTED FOR HENRY COLBURN,
PUBLIC LIBRARY, CONDUIT STREET, HANOVER SQUARE.
1816.

B. Clarke, Printer, Well-Street, London.

DEDICATION.

TO

WILLIAM GIFFORD, Esq.

&c. &c. &c.

Sir,

Your acceptance of the following trifle will much oblige me. I know no one to whom I could offer it with more propriety than to you, who have the happiness of conducting a publication, the most important both for the correction and encouragement of science, literature, morals, and politics, that has ever appeared in this kingdom. Mine is but a light-armed auxiliary; yet even as such, it may not be without its use.

I am, Sir,

With great truth,

Your most humble,

And obedient Servant,

THE AUTHOR.

PREFACE.

SOME years ago, I lifted my pen against a certain Ministry, who had just declared that they united in themselves "All the talent, weight, and consideration of the country." Very soon afterwards, I chaunted their departing requiem. Accustomed to those chicaning arts, which are acquired by a long course of Opposition, they had presented a paper for the royal signature, quite different from the commands, and diametrically opposite to the known sentiments of the King, in the humble hope that His Majesty would sign it without perusal. His Majesty, however, was aware that attornies sometimes foist a false deed upon an honest man, and thus make him sign away a whole estate; he, therefore, read the paper, discovered the forgery, and dismissed the perpetrators.

After this disgrace, they remained, for some years, quite stupified; until at length, the murder of a minister inspired them with new hopes and expectations. They had formerly tried to swindle their King, and they now boasted that they would bully their Prince. They thought all sure; they dictated terms, ran wild through the streets, met, smirked, winked, shook hands, made out a complete list of ministry, and were sent about their business.

Ever since that period, they have cherished an inveterate hatred against royalty. All that men could do to render the Regent odious, they have done; from the British lordling, who oratorized on ormolu, to the Scotch commoner, who hinted at decapitation. If they could not prove his infringement upon the laws, they could, at least, assert his deviation from good taste; and when Magna Charta failed them, they had recourse to a cupola and a dragon. Then, his uniform was unconstitutional, and he gave a ball and supper; and he had gold fishes, and he had a fashionable coat, and he had personal friends, and he had ministers who were not the ministers that ought to be the ministers; and he had an opposition who were not the opposition that ought to be the opposition; and, therefore, this opposition held cabals, and brought out a newspaper, and hired libellers, and spies, and hissers, and hooters, and demireps, and perjurers; and insinuated what they dared not assert, and asserted what they could not prove, and proved what was nothing to the purpose; and could not get into place after all!

This plot had not even the merit of originality. It was borrowed from the French Regicides. Poissardism against the Capets gave rise to Billinsgate against the Brunswicks.

In fact, there was always, and is still, an alarming coincidence of sentiment between the regicides and the Foxites. Radical reform became the common cry of both. Corresponding societies united both in fraternal amity. We may trace the fondness of both for another French Revolution, in the remonstrance against our protection of Louis from insurrections, and in the late attempt at Grenoble. Fraternal amity, too, is still observable in the kind interference for aliens.

Even the best of the Foxites could never see the true cause and object of the war. They merely considered it as a very serious dispute about treaties and territories—as a most important affair of posts. But never could they be persuaded to believe that it was a contest of anarchy against order, of infidelity against religion, and of innovating theory against established truth. They had not the least idea that opinion, education, social duty, and domestic happiness, were depending upon the result. If they *had* any such idea, they were traitors.

Mr. Pitt owed, and his successors still owe, their political ascendancy to their early and undeviating conviction of the real nature of the struggle. It is quite impossible that the party now in power, could, for so many years, have retained their situations, if public opinion had not supported them throughout. A parliament which forsook them on a question, where a few millions only were concerned, would hardly have countenanced them in the expenditure of hundreds of millions, had it conceived that the war was either unnecessary or misconducted; or had it felt a greater confidence in any other set of men. I am sure I do not intend to represent either Mr. Pitt or his successors as faultless. I merely mean to shew, that the nation approved of them, because their general principles, and general conduct, appeared praiseworthy. A peace dictated in the capital of our deadly foe, is some set-off against the interference of a few horsemen at a levee.

I protest, I had no notion of intruding upon the Talents again, till their late attempts determined me. Foreseeing that peace would annihilate several very turbulent questions, and leave ministers in undisturbed repose, they have made one last and desperate effort to persuade the nation, that its temporary distresses (the result of a long war) are inherent and perpetual.

Though the clouds have dispersed, and the winds are silent, they point, with a savage joy, at the unsubsided waves. It is their mean, and unmanly, and unstatesman-like deportment; it is—for I may carp upon this point, since even a pavillion undergoes their atticism;—it is their want of *taste* in scurrility which has moved me. Neither can I permit their initiated accomplices to go unbranded. These new men are almost as troublesome as the old. Some of them, indeed, promised better things, till bad company corrupted them; so, having preferred the poisoned shirt of Nessus to the skin of the Nemæan lion, they must suffer for their choice. But though they may feel the torture of Hercules, they shall not commit his devastation.

THE TALENTS RUN MAD;*

OR,

Eighteen Hundred and Sixteen.

DIALOGUE THE FIRST.

FRIEND.

HEALTH, and what news?

AUTHOR.

You banter.—Pray, forbear
That venerable question, now so rare.

---

* I have given my book this title, because the persons whom it celebrates are really in a dreadful state of mind at present. After contending twenty years against ministers, who had, not alone them, but France to combat, just conceive what they must now feel at seeing France on a sudden overturned, and themselves left to carry on the war single-handed! How heart-rending! I protest I am not at all surprised at their derangement. Fortunately for WHITBREAD and WYNDHAM, they did not live to witness the discomfiture. SH-R---N too—he seems out of the scrape, and remains, I am told, in the full possession of his faculties. But poor GR-Y is now beyond the power even of another war to tranquillize. As for T--RN-Y, he both rages and jests in a way shocking to humanity. Desperation sits somewhat easier on GR-NV-LLE; and L-NSD--NE merely breaks out into a waltz. But there is a sweet me-

France conquer'd, Europe peaceful, England crown'd
With reeking laurels, where can news abound?

---

lancholy about P-ns--by, which almost makes him interesting; and I know not what beautiful distraction it is which so happily harmonizes with the soft features of Br——m. These sufferers still frequent St. Stephens's, as usual; but their situation is respected. There they mechanically repeat their old predictions about our ruin; which, however, they now derive from a complete new set of causes. The principal of these are, a cottage, a life-guardsman, and a secretary. Indeed, they likewise shew remarkable madness in their anxiety to overrun the country with aliens, and to prevent British officers from dining together. But I will dwell no longer on their unhappy state. It is cruel to excite ridicule when the object deserves commiseration. Out of charity, therefore, I shall henceforth treat them as men, who merely do mischief with all their senses about them.

France conquer'd.]—'The conquest of France!' exclaimed Fox, in his address, 'The conquest of France! O calumniated crusaders; how rational and moderate were your objects! O much-injured Louis XIV. upon what slight grounds have you been accused of restless and immoderate ambition! O tame and feeble Cervantes, with what a timid pencil and faint colours have you painted the portrait of a disordered imagination!'

The prophecy of Fox! O calumniated Joanna Southcote, how rational and moderate were your predictions! O much injured Napoleon Buonaparte, upon what slight grounds have you been accused of false and daring prognostication! O tame and feeble Machiavel, with what a timid pencil and faint colours have you painted the portrait of a perverted politician!

FRIEND.

What then, must Peace extend her sleepy power,
O'er stocks and C--HR-NE, B-RD-TT and the Tower?
Are no dice extant? Is Brookes' temple too
To Janus' turned? Are hose no longer blue?
Is royal slander dumb? Lo! France can screen
Caught wives; and anvill'd Gretna yet is green.

AUTHOR.

Yes, vice and folly still untam'd will prove;
Wigs will grow trim on consistorial love.

O'er stocks and C--HR-NE.]—His Lordship, it seems, is resolved on bringing forward his case every year. Does he then hope to convince the world of his innocence by adding to his notoriety? Weak men sometimes (Sir FR-NC-S always) will believe even the most detected culprit innocent; but the fact is, my Lord, not one in ten thousand doubts the justice of your sentence. Pray, then, do not tease us about it. You have no chance, I tell you, till the old major gets us a reform; and he has found that a thirty years' business already.

Is royal slander dumb?]—I suppose my friend alludes to that detestable conspiracy, which was organized, some time since, against the personal character of the Regent. It is now completely detected, and so are all those villains, who, under the specious name of *advisers*, were the prime movers of it. They know this well; they know too, that they must henceforth expect no favor; and hence their diatribes against royalty, hence their disgusting struggles between treason and cowardice, hence that melancholy spectacle, which, night, after night they still exhibit, of defiance in fetters and emaciated desperation.

If our king added twenty isles before,
Great —— will engraft two buttons more.

Great —— will engraft two buttons more.]—An elderly young gentleman of twenty years' practice in the ton. Since he will not reform our dress, I wish our patriots would do something for it. Considering we live at such epic times, our costume is sadly deficient in the picturesque. Future ages will read with astonishment, that the wisest schemes were planned, and the most gigantic feats executed, by people in smart coats with a dangling shred of skirt, bandages round their necks, and—I tremble to write the word—breeches! For goodness' sake, how is a poet, five centuries hence, to manage about the battle of Waterloo? Instead of hacked hauberks and habergeons, perforated mail, and arrows stuck in shields, he must sing of holes made in pantaloons, jackets shot away, and little buttons that stop a bullet. Or will antiquity itself, by association of ideas, give a venerable effect to the word knapsack, or add sublimity to the word canteen? In my opinion, epic poets are undone. It will be still worse with painters. Flaps and tags, buckles and pumps, may, hereafter, as obsolete terms, acquire some degree of dignity; but I fear, no sleight of pencil can ever make a cocked hat harmonize with horror. In poetry, we conceive a grand idea of Satan, when we read,

——' On his crest
Sat horror plum'd——'

But reduce the image to canvas—paint horror fairly perched upon his crest, and the fact is, you must either make her so small as to look like any thing but horror, or so large as to dwindle the devil into a mere dwarf. In short, our present costume is a disgrace to heroism, and I am astonished the opposition do not take the matter up.

And dames, whose tongues would Babel's own o'er-
pow'r,
Will make their bonnets imitate its tower.
With broomsticks Er—NE still shall grace our soot,
Our stage be still invaded dog and foot.

They who made so grand a stand on military mustachios, tassels, and heavy helmets, might surely go one step farther, and rectify the errors of the civil wardrobe. In truth, it would set ministers at their wits' ends, were a motion made, some night or other, for leave to bring in a bill *for the regulation of the dress of his Majesty's liege subjects, in a manner suitable to the dignity of the country, and to the high station which it holds amongst the other powers of Europe.*

Will make their bonnets imitate its tower.]—I had intended a long note upon the female costume of the present day; but unfortunately, the little milliner who promised me her assistance has just eloped with a sentimental pugilist. I can, therefore, only venture to regret, that the face, which formerly used to crown the whole edifice, is now (between short petticoats and tall bonnets) stuck just in the centre of the dress, like a clock on a steeple; and that the waist is so plaited and puckered (I trust I speak technically,) that we can only point it out, as we might other culprits—to the best of our belief.

N. B. The pretty little Grecian bend forward of the spine (adopted, I presume, from the Venus) is quite classical and broken-backed.

With broomsticks Er—NE still shall grace our soot.]—His Lordship, it is well known, was lately convicted of selling birch-brooms. It is not quite so well known, that the culprit walked three miles to make a pun (which in-

Still too, some crowing curricle, I trust,
Will figure 8 on fashionable dust;
While lily shallows to fools' caps aspire,
And H— and Dick contend for names of fire;
And clubs, from catchpoles whipping four in hand,
Hold oaths as nothing, but make wagers stand.

---

deed deserved the birch) upon his own conviction. His guilt being decided by a clause, he called it a *sweeping clause!* As I have inserted this *Jeu d'esprit*, I know his Lordship will forgive me all I may say of him afterwards.

And H— and Dick contend for names of fire.]—Hell-fire Dick, a noted coachman of Oxford, and the most agreeable whip (as he himself undertakes to inform us), " that ever drove under the trees, or over the houses."

Four in hand.]—I wish these worthy fellows, who live upon their dickies, to know (what I dare say will astonish them), that there is much patriotism, as well as virtue, in their occupation. I verily believe we owed our quadrupedal superiority in Spain and France to that useful class of gentlemen, who cultivate a friendship with their horses; and no doubt, Christian humility could not be more pleasingly displayed than in their condescending to the connection. Indeed, horses, at all periods, have formed no inconsiderable link in the social chain. A whole property sometimes depends upon a single horse. A horse has his doctor—a far more scientific personage than the mere physician, because, as the patient in hoofs cannot conveniently turn pale or sport a pulse, the symptoms are more difficult of discovery. Caligula, we know, gave his horse an ivory manger. Heroes have their statues stuck upon horses. Achilles (like our own gentlemen) talked greatly to his horse; and it is an ascertained fact, that a lady often de-

FRIEND.

In England, pregnant with increasing crimes,
New æras have effac'd the good old times.

AUTHOR.

In England, nurse of virtue more than ill,
Old times were good, but new are better still.

FRIEND.

How? Better!

AUTHOR.

Prove them worse.

FRIEND.

Our riches view:
Wealth begets luxury.

---

cides which man she will marry, merely by the number of his horses.

Old times were good, but new are better still.]—' Good old times,' is an expression, I presume, as old as a century after the deluge. Men look back upon the past as upon a mountain, which appears the more blue and smooth, the more distant it becomes. But I have no hesitation to say, that this country now stands higher in point of morals and true piety than it ever stood before. This improvement arises, as I conceive, from our gradual progress in knowledge, from the corrective influence of a pure religion and a free constitution, from our political seclusion during a whole age, and from the tremendous spectacle of other nations; by whose crimes, as we did not participate in them, we must naturally have benefitted. A signal example of depravity makes a certain impression upon every spectator; and if it does not act as an encouragement, it must operate as a warning.

AUTHOR.

And knowledge too;
And knowledge virtue. Go, that period boast,
When more than London's arch one Bible cost;
And censure days, with wealth and learning fraught,
When all may Bibles buy and all have bought.

FRIEND.

When tradesmen chariots sport—

AUTHOR.

And purses give,
That the poor ravag'd Leipsickers may live.

FRIEND.

Half give for popular applause.

AUTHOR.

Sure sign,
To charity the public thoughts incline;
Since those whose god is men's opinions, swerve
From selfish nature, for the god they serve.

FRIEND.

Yet see, what waste of wealth! Pagodas rise;
Thatcht cots and gilt pavillions fright our eyes!

When more than London's arch one Bible cost.]—The rebuilding of an arch (indeed, I believe, two arches) of London Bridge cost but twenty-nine pounds at a time when a M. S. Bible (for printing had not then been invented) amounted to much the same sum.

Pagodas rise; thatcht cots and gilt pavillions fright our eyes.]—If, as the cabal assert, the prince sacrifices public

AUTHOR.

When fishmongers build castles, for a king
To build a cot, is no such mighty thing.
But oh, how CR-VY, M-LT-N, M--RE would stun,
If Windsor's mile of towers were now begun!

---

good to personal prodigality, it is astonishing that he should never have chosen for his ministers those men who formerly worked heaven and earth to procure him liberal supplies from parliament. What ingratitude!—As for royal expence, the Duke de Berri alone has a larger income than any four of our own princes; and the British throne and court cost less than those of the first-rate powers in Europe, and not more than several of the second-rate. Still, talk of expenditure to the cabal, and 'tis nothing but, the Prince, the Prince, the Prince. The Prince has misapplied the public money. What money? The Droits of Admiralty? No, but the salaries of ministers. He has given them to mere loyal men, instead of Jacobins. This is the true secret, why he who was once the darling of opposition, has now become its utter aversion. I remember reading of a Russian Princess who had a crucifix which she used to worship with kisses, genuflections, and lighted tapers, 'provided always' she was in a good humour. But if any thing cross occurred; if a rival eclipsed her, or an admirer grew cool, no lip-service or prostration then; out went the tapers in a pet, and the crucifix got well scolded.

Cr-vy.]—An ironical gentleman of the house, with, however, considerable dullness in the didactic. When he speaks, if our mouths are not distended horizontally in laughter, they are sure to assume the perpendicularity of a yawn. He was convicted of a libel.

Yet England now could purchase England then,
Ten times, and leave behind another ten.
Haste then, ye stables, ask the lord's assent;
Ye pigsties rise by act of parliament!

FRIEND.

Yet mark the stripling, patriarch, virgin, dame;
All they abhor in guilt is feeling shame.
The husband drives by his indebted door,
His mistress, faithful as his spouse, or more.
Bloods in a duel jest while taking lives,
And greybeards, for a wager, ruin wives.
While fair fifteen comes pasted with a bloom
From France, and garters in the drawing-room.

M-LT-N.]—What quixotism possessed his Lordship, who, it seems, is a mighty good sort of young man, to go careering against a guardsman? I am told he copies Mr. Pitt's language. I wish he would imitate Mr. Pitt's dignity. That great statesman would not, I rather suspect, have gone *careering*.

M—RE.]—Master Peter. He talks now and then. They say too he reads a great deal. If so, *nobody* is the wiser.

Garters in the drawing-room.]—At least, some of our young ladies do not scruple to shew knees in French drawing-rooms. No doubt they will shortly let their own countrymen have a peep. It would be but friendly. In fact, we must bear patiently with such follies, till the travelling fit is over. Every one now returns from abroad, either Beparised or Bewaterlooed. I have seen a hulking fellow, hot from a fortnight's trip, sacre Dieu it, and grin it, and shrug it, with the most serious intentions of ele-

Because a horse's head has reach'd a post
Late by three inches, an estate is lost.
Two wheels succeed to four, dice shake, and then
The wheel of fortune gives four wheels again.
One, to trap wealth, adulterates youthful minds,
And in that process half his pleasure finds.
The joys of life, wine, mistresses and friends,
He makes them means, as others make them ends;
Pursu'd and valu'd with no other aim,
Than just to further some ensnaring game.
Bill-trusting waiters can his bow command,
And swindlers honor him with half a hand.
One shuns our fair ones' European charms,
And woos the brown embrace of Afric arms.

---

gance. Others, again, stun you with no account whatever of La Belle Alliance; and I know one honest gentleman, who has brought home a real Waterloo thumb, nail and all, which he preserves in a bottle of gin, for the purpose of transmitting, to the most remote posterity, a relic of Sawney Mac Gregor from Inverness, or of Darby O'Rourke from Tipperary.

Woos the brown embrace of Afric arms.]—It is well known, that divers gentlemen, stricken in years, paid the most delicate attentions to the Hottentot Venus. As for that idle story of the good Mr. B——, no one now believes a syllable of it. The facts of the interview were these. Mr. B—— having called on Venus, naturally began the conversation by remarking that it was a fine day. Venus agreed with him; and no sooner did she observe that the day before had also been fine, than he agreed with her.

Another, scorning modest hearts to move,
Tries to make brawling hags run mad with love.
  Yes, in vile London all is base or quaint;
Fops upon crutches, pugilists who paint.
There the white pageant meets the blacken'd pall;
There bishops clap the palm while Tuscans squall;
Or, napkin'd for the knife, with nostril near,
Say half a grace upon the tainted deer.
All are deprav'd: even fighting shopboys know
Chalk Farm, and butchers' daughters read Rousseau.

AUTHOR.

Judge not by private vice; the nation scan.
Why trades she not in marketable man?
Why sends she presents of the real god,
To climes where Christian foot had never trod?
What chastens even her stage? What bids encrease
Her pious writings, and her impious cease?
And why, mistrustful of the world around,
Fled to her honest hearth three kings uncrown'd?

He then took the opportunity of hoping that the next day might be as fine; and she did not omit so favorable an occasion of likewise hoping that it might. In short, there was not a drop of rain difference in their opinions; and Mr. B—— concluded a conversation, replete with weather, by converting Venus to Christianity.

Fled to her honest hearth three kings uncrown'd.]—Namely—Louis, Gustavus, and Napoleon.

These are grand features; these her outline grace,
Tho' warts and freckles still deform her face;
Tho' W-TH-N still has shouts, and D-X-N sneers;
Tho' dukes are grooms and statesmen charioteers.

FRIEND.

You praise our godly—What! th' exclusive sect,
Born ready sav'd, and preordain'd elect?
What! jumpers, Southcotes, saints, and millenarians,
Supralapsarians, nay, and Sublapsarians.
What! kissers, antikissers, dunkers, shakers,
Celestial grocers, superhuman bakers;

Jumpers.]—A Welsh sect, who piously leap about till they drop. He who can leap the longest is considered the best jumper; and therefore the most muscular men have the greatest chance of eternal beatitude. Their arguments in favour of jumping are, that David danced before the Ark, that the babe leaped in the womb of Elizabeth, and that the lame man leaped in praise of God.

Southcotes.]—One of poor Joanna's followers was caught in the fact of bargaining for a Young Shiloh with a Wiltshire woman who had twins. Joanna's only real miracle was the conversion of certain illuminati to a belief in her mumming mystics. I wonder what those divine mantua-makers have done with the baby linen?

Supralapsarians, nay, and Sublapsarians.]—The supras assert that God merely *permitted* Adam to transgress. The subs hold, that his fall was foredoomed from all eternity.

Kissers.]—A sect who take sly advantage of some scriptural phrase, to kiss when they meet. It naturally enough consists of old maids and young widows. The seceding

Blest with the true gogonianting tone,
Grins of all curl and every tribe of groan.
Prim, furious, solemn, pert, unshorn, unshod,
All hating churchmen for the love of God.

---

antikissers were established by certain morose husbands and fathers.

Dunkers.]—An American sect who sleep upon trunks of trees, and starve themselves to the bone. Our LORD MAYOR is no Dunker. TH--RPE, who would be an Alderman, is no Dunker. ALDERMAN G—DB—RE is no Dunker.

Shakers.]—Another sect remarkable for agility. They pique themselves particularly upon spinning round for an hour or two; which, they say, shews the great power of God.

Celestial Grocers, Superhuman Bakers.]—There is a publication called the Methodists' Magazine, which, on the whole, is neither injurious nor uninstructive; but for a thing of its pretensions, singularly tinctured with the *vanitas vanitatis*. There, evangelical tradesmen insert their own memoirs, as avowed patterns of piety; and indeed, better creatures, they tell you, never breathed. Others again get their faces affixed to the work, though, I trust, not from vanity; for a set of uglier christians were never beheld. Besides, the language is often carnal and prophane to a degree. Why talk of wrestling with Our Saviour? Why call spiritual meetings, love feasts? The poor creatures mean well, but they disgust persons of plain piety. And yet this work is patronized, nay superintended, by men of education and talents.

The true gogonianting tone.]—Gogoniant, in the Welsh, signifies glory. The Welsh preachers instruct their flocks to keep bellowing it till their lungs fail them.

All worshipping, not graven figures quite,
But an odd sort of metaphoric light.
Nay, think, th' elect behold it!

AUTHOR.

Psha, at dark,
Some knuckle from their optics struck a spark.
Much I condemn these call'd and sected schools,
These pious mischiefs of well-meaning fools.
Yet few their numbers. Saints, methinks, withdraw,
Not from the church, but her neglected law.

Nay, think, th' elect behold it.]—In the Methodists' Magazine, a self-biographer assures us that he prayed one night till his chamber became illuminated! There was one Quirinus Kuhlman, who used to imagine that a globe of divine light always surrounded his head. Accordingly, he wrote books upon eternal keys and padlocks, and was fried to death for his pains.

Saints, methinks, withdraw; not from the church but her neglected law.]—I certainly respect that class of men who, without forsaking the regular church, exert themselves as individuals, to promote christian knowledge. So far from injuring the religion of the state, they serve it essentially, by animating the ardour of our divines. They rouse zeal without exciting rancour, and cause discussion without propagating fanaticism. I am, however, far from intending to cast any slur upon the clergy. They are the most respectable and learned body of men in the kingdom; and their writings have latterly thrown so important a light upon passing events, that even legislators might study them with advantage.

Indeed, I must say of the saints, (as they are called,)

Strict to her tenets, such would but restore
That discipline she better taught before.

FRIEND.

Well then, these saints, I reckon, can endure
Hard-pinching thrift, and patiently be poor.
Lo! Peace appears: but say, what pomp attends?
None, save a troop of shoulder-tapping friends.

---

that they sometimes carry their enthusiasm and their strictness to excess. Thus, I cannot, for my life, see the mischief arising from theatres. If we are not to frequent places of instruction, because we may also encounter scenes of depravity, we cannot stir outside our doors. Vice may assail us even on our way to church. Thus too, in Cœlebs, young ladies (on the principle, I think, of preventing vain thoughts) are advised not to work dresses for themselves, but only for their friends. I would improve upon the hint. Instead of spots and festoons, they should work nothing except scriptural patterns. A border of deluge would run prettily enough round a miss's frock; and a set of scornful Josephs, embroidered on a lady's tucker, might often preserve it from molestation.

Lo, Peace appears.]—Opposition have often told us that we live in a new æra. There is no doubt of the fact; for never was a country, till now, ruined by peace and plenty! After all, England must be a most extraordinary creature. War is to undo her, Peace is to undo her, Plenty is to undo her. *Is* to undo her? She is undone. *Is* undone? She has actually been undone then twenty years. These twenty years has she been as poor as a rat. And yet, under all this poverty, she has fought the whole world, beaten the whole world, and saved the whole

Much-slander'd friends, who with encreasing zeal,
When all else fly, still follow at our heel.
Make shift with palaces, ye vulgar sort!
Jails are the houses of polite resort.
Men of champaign were ton in former time;
Now bankrupts are bang-up, and debtors prime.
A standing army, and a warlike peace!
Poor England, who but sees thy swift decease?

AUTHOR.

'Tis the last bar of one unwearied song,
That now has quaver'd twenty sessions long.
Nay, 'tis a national old tune, I trow.
Whole centuries back sang 'England down must go.'

---

world; and now here she stands, alive and well! Oh, but then, her national debt—think of that, Master Brook! 'Tis monstrous, I grant you; but if she had never incurred it, she had now been in her grave. Indeed, certain people are rather angry that she did not save both herself and the whole human race for nothing. 'There goes the rascal who cut off my arm!' said a fellow. 'Your arm? how shocking! What on earth possessed him?' 'Why, to save my life.' 'Well then, he has saved it.' 'But dont you see he has cut off my arm?' 'Nay but—' 'What signify buts? He has cut off my arm—that is enough—he has cut off my arm!'

Whole centuries back sang 'England down must go.']—In the reign of Charles the Second, a pamphlet, called 'Britannia Languens,' was written, which proved, to a factious demonstration, that England could not possibly hold out ten years longer!

Disband! What now, while France yet terror spreads?
Ere crowns are warm on rein ted heads?
While all beside stand armed?

FRIEND.

Yet freedom fails
Each empire, where a soldiery prevails.

AUTHOR.

Then, if we must, in mercy, let us fall,
By our own armies, not the hounds of Gaul.
The crown our soldiers took, themselves restor'd,
The foreign Saxon kept both crown and sword.
Go then, like GR–NV–E, sell our naval store,
And war may catch us naked as before.
For come war must. 'Tis vain to lull alarm.
Imps shall go forth and Armageddon arm.

Like GR-NV-LLE, sell our naval store.]--After the peace of Amiens, his Lordship innocently sold off the contents of our naval arsenals; and to whom, think you? Why, to France! The consequence was, that when war broke out again, we found ourselves destitute of every material necessary for our navy.

For come war must.]—No man can pretend to foretell how long peace may continue; but this every man must know, that all those feelings and principles and objects which have agitated mankind during the last fifty years, still remain unsubdued. 'Men gnaw their tongues for pain, and repent not of their deeds.' There is but a murmuring calmness. A spark may yet light a flame which an ocean cannot extinguish. Meantime, our wisest method of averting

Not yet has Heaven its mighty havoc done,
Not all its vengeful vials yet have run.
Old feuds still lurk beneath this calm repose,
And some dread hour their relics shall disclose.
So the lone traveller in Egypt sees,
A sandy desert smooth without a breeze.
But winds awake; the sands in eddies fly,
Or roll in waves and whirl along the sky.
Till one tremendous blast sweeps all away,
And lo, a field of carnage meets the day!
Ten thousand ghastly warriors smeared with gore;
And fresh the battle lies that bled an age before.

---

the evil day, is by shewing ourselves prepared to receive it. The hand is upon the hilt throughout Europe. Those who hold only the shield, must fall by the sword.

END OF DIALOGUE THE FIRST.

DIALOGUE THE SECOND.

FRIEND.

I MARVEL much, since times like these awake
Mens' minds, why genius should our realm forsake.
Past years o'erflow'd with heroes, and with wits.
Where are our Nelsons, Cowpers, Foxs, Pitts?

AUTHOR.

Thus other ages too will mourn their lots:
'Where are our Wellesleys, Currans, Stewarts, Scotts?'
Men own not talents until talents end.
Who deems a genius none? His dearest friend.
Because they liv'd and school'd and play'd like brother;
As if one's dullness could infect the other.

FRIEND.

Yet see, 'tis Ireland each high badge displays.
Thus Wellington the truncheon, Moore the bays,

Curran.]—The great orator of the Irish bar. I have heard both him and LORD ER—NE often, and can affirm, that in sublime, pathetic, and effective eloquence, Curran is superior beyond all comparison.

Moore the bays.]—My friend places Moore before Scott and Lord Byron, just as one would prefer Anacreon to Statius or Apollonius Rhodius. Because, though amatory

And Castlereagh the robe.—Or would you steal
From actual life to mimic?—see O'Neill.

---

poetry is of a less exalted species than epic, one would rather excel in the minor department, than be secondary in the superior.

Castlereagh the robe.]—I hesitate to praise a prime minister; but this I may say, without being convicted of eulogy, that his Lordship has acquired the full confidence of the nation at large. This, in fact, is every thing.

See O'Neill.]—I have heard people of the finest taste and feeling declare, that they would never go to see this lady perform again. In fact, they felt so much affected, that they dreaded to suffer another such night of tears. Her powers in the pathetic, are, indeed, wonderful.

I wish a national theatre, with opera hours and prices, were established at the west end of the town, and then, perhaps, our fashionables would condescend to patronize a place of rational amusement. At present, the opera, or rather the ballet, engrosses all their favor; for though they are content with *seeing* the singers, they must *hear* the dancers. The moment the ballet begins, an instantaneous silence reigns through the house. Not a billet-doux can drop from a dowager unheard; so great is the respect paid to the majesty of toes. Occasional whispers, however, are ventured now and then. Vestris, for instance, is observed to be in much limb, as he has spun round once and a segment more than usual. Then the eloquence of an attitude, or the pathos of a pas de seul, is superb; and certain old cognoscenti admire the keeping of the groups of flower girls. Some of them, indeed, are kept long enough, as one may see by their wrinkles, while the fatness of others shews plainly, that they are, at least, kept well.

AUTHOR.

The deeds of Wellington, unconquer'd lord!
Let written fire on adamant record.
A Scipio rescuing Rome from punic flame,
At the last gasp of conquer'd worlds he came.
Sedate in danger, cautious, and yet warm,
Prompt to decide and mighty to perform;
Swift as the lightning his resolve was given,
Destruction follow'd, like the bolt of Heaven.
When all seem'd lost, serene he dar'd contend,
And boldly made even danger's self his friend:
Saw where the dawning of the victory lay,
And snatch'd th' immortal crisis from the day.

FRIEND.

Sc–tt is no poet.

AUTHOR.

That I greatly doubt;
Tho' far we read to find the poet out.
Bid him contract.—The Sybil's books of yore,
As less their number grew, were valu'd more.

Bid him contract.]—I hope Mr. Sc-tt, (of whose powers I have a high opinion) will not consider me an enemy for giving him good advice. But, really, authors, now-a-days, write by the pound or by the foot. Mr. Sc-tt, I think, has dropped a good many of his wis's, and weens, and by my fays; neither has he yet adopted the new fashion of *sanctifying* his words. Saith for said, spake for spoke, brake for broke, unto for to, doth for does, are the ca-

FRIEND.

Well, B–R–N SC–TT excels.

AUTHOR.

In shorter song;
And shorter still would still the praise prolong.
But how would praise transcend, if like a ball,
His verses came to have no length at all!

---

priccios of the day. I likewise see just cause and impediment against such marriages as, war-storm, death-storm, battle-fire. The best authorities for which are, pot-hooks, kitchen-stuff, cabbage-garden.

B-R-N SC-TT excels.]—I differ from my friend decidedly. Lord B-R-N is a metaphysician, not a poet. SC-TT is to him, what Thompson is to Young. The one excels in describing things, the other in delineating thoughts. If the one swims too much on the surface, the other is overloaded and sinks too deep. Of SC-TT, we seldom read a line twice, (though we may a passage) because he wants force; or of B-R-N, because he wants poetry. By poetry, I mean that nameless charm of expression, which raises it above prose. Whenever his Lordship tries metaphor, he fails most miserably. Take for instance, this distich.

'May the strong curse of crusht affections light
Back on thy bosom with reflected blight.'

Really, this is the most extraordinary curse (and in more ways than one) that ever came from the pen of a poet. It is a curse, in short, which first turns into a ray, then sets off from a bosom, returns back, becomes a flower, and at last suffers a curious blight enough,—a *reflected blight.* Now a flower which reflects, can, I think, be no other than Venus's looking-glass.

FRIEND.

Ay, B-R-N stung you.

AUTHOR.

Happy I to raise
His censure, but protect me from his praise!
Where'er his beam of approbation burns,
Sour at the touch, each milky virtue turns.
Of this convinc'd, and having wreaked his worst,
He kindly libels all he lauded first.
Even kindred blood his praise once underwent;
But slander came, so uncle sat content.
In eight dull lines he bade a princess weep.
Strange! when he counsell'd tears, to give one sleep.
Leave English, B-R-N; ay, and England too.
The Persic-Turcic-Arabic for you.
Buy an Ionian Isle, there naturalize
Old words, and with seraglios colonize.

Ay, B-R-N stung you.]—

'On 'All the talents' vent your *venal* spleen;
Want your defence, let pity be your screen.'
English Bards and Scotch Reviewers.

After these unfounded personalities, his Lordship can expect no mercy from *me*. I, however, have less occasion than others to complain of his licentious satire. His 'Sketch from Private Life' draws a portrait so diabolical, that I defy it to find a prototype in nature; and if it be meant for any human being, I thank my God I have not a heart capable of suggesting such vengeance, far less of laying the demoniac anatomy bare to the public gaze.

There question if the bed be damp, or whether
The stream be cool—not common talk of weather.
Bard of the bùlbul, (oh, poetic sound!)
Sing how, when friends desert, tame bears are found.
Or sing Leander swimming four-mile heats,
Or how divinely well snake-porridge eats.
Seven waistcoats wear, run fifteen miles on foot,
For fatness to some brains is glue to soot.
Else go, unlearn your learning, or add more.
Not what Greece is, but what she was before.
If you draw heroes from your kindred mind,
Transplant them, leave no duplicate behind.
Last, keep your friendly promise to be dumb,
And some fine morning common sense may come.
More would you seek? Yes, something more you want;
You left your neckcloth in the Hellespont.

FRIEND.

Forbear.

AUTHOR.

I spare him.—Hark! a Pasha sings;
Love is his descant, yet his descant stings.
Quite smooth, it paints him to distraction driven;
Asks pardon so as ne'er to be forgiven;

There question if the bed be damp, or whether the stream be cool.]—In Italy the nightly question is, 'have you sprinkled the bed?' In Cumana, the first question in the morning is, 'have we a cool river to-day?'

Gives an unmanly deed a warbling grace,
And daggers with affectionate grimace.
Why turns he infidel? Because 'tis odd.
'Midst all his libels he must libel God.
Yet still his pen leaves some things undisgrac'd,
For vice he holds essential to good taste;
And sure his curse no lady e'er receives,
Sent only to that hell he disbelieves.
Worse mischief lurks in his didactic air.
When the fox preaches, let the fowl beware.
Stern boy! whom nought but discontent can please;
Made barbarous by refinement, fierce by ease;
Why flies he where no lowering clouds deform?
How can the seagull scream without a storm?
Let wings angelic guard him as he flies,
Crop them he cannot, but will satirize.
Place him in Heaven, (poetic licence may,)
His soul will mutter at eternal day.

FRIEND.

Enough.—And now propound, what I foresee,
Will rack your faculties—tho' thirty-three;

Will rack your faculties, tho' thirty-three.]—Spurzeim, the man of skulls, has accommodated the human race with thirty-three faculties. His theory would be quite established, if he could prove that he himself possesses half the number.

Why, 'mid this lamentable dearth of brain,
Still 'all the talents' unemployed remain?

AUTHOR.

In popular states, where each has equal chance,
Mean genius sinks and worthier parts advance.
Shake in a vessel shot of different size,
The larger mounts, the less at bottom lies.
Should men who France invincible believ'd,
Conduct a warfare they so misconceiv'd?
Should prophets, who to Spain foreboded ill,
Get pow'r, and thus their prophecies fulfil?

ALL THE TALENTS.]—I take some merit to myself for having made this a Cabalistical term, and fixed it on these folks in perpetuity. But really 'tis quite delightful to hear them still talking of their talents, and of the confidence which the country feels in their powers of legislation. Why a whole generation—the third part of the people—have grown up under the present government. They know nothing about opposition as a ministry; save and except one disastrous trial of a year, a month and a day. Nine years, however, have since elapsed, without the least danger of another trial, even for an hour, a minute and a second.

Prophets, who to Spain foreboded ill.]—No man can now deny that it was the Spanish war which saved Europe. And here I must say a few words about the Spanish patriots. If ever we were justified in interfering between a government and its subjects, we should act as mediators for these unfortunate men. We fought conjointly with them, when their avowed object was constitutional, as well as national liberty. That liberty they have not ob-

For they, without reserve, would mischief do,
To make the mischief they predicted true.
Full twenty years, mere critics, they revile
By system, and each session plot their style.
Learn why the nation more confides in those
Who govern, than who twenty years oppose.
Good measures are mens' interest, when in place.
Outs hold it their's good measures to disgrace.
Tho' England suffer'd, outs would chuckle still,
For their own sakes, should ministers act ill.
A priest once cross'd the seas, inform'd before,
Not to fear dnger while the sailors swore.
A storm arose; they curs'd their souls to hell,
And the priest prais'd his god they curs'd so well!

---

tained, but are exiled. Can we not possibly influence Ferdinand in the adoption of such a system as might unite both parties? This I know, that to preserve Spain from a civil war is our interest; and that the patriots, if not conciliated, may shake the Spanish throne to its foundation. At all events, as a mere matter of feeling, we should undertake the cause of our old companions in arms.

Good measures are men's interest when in place.]—Common sense, self-love, and even chance, all conspire to make a minister act for the public good. As often, therefore, as he does right, a systematical opposition must do wrong. Now in all human calculation, a minister, so actuated, must do right three times for once that he does wrong; and consequently, a systematical opposition must do wrong three times for once that it does right.

FRIEND.

Gr-y, grant, is a deserving man at least.

AUTHOR.

Man! recollect he calls himself a beast.
Once, rough-shod, he would tramp up Carlton stairs.
How well this packhorse disappointment bears!

FRIEND.

Man? Horse? say Sagittarius.

AUTHOR.

Ay, no doubt,
One of twelve signs that talent must stay out.

FRIEND.

Eleven then still remain.

AUTHOR.

Six only thrive.
Death, voters, and disgust subtracted five.
Poor Sherry—

FRIEND.

Nay, let him, without controul,
Still circulate the peremptory bowl;

Once, rough-shod, he would tramp up Carlton stairs.]—'Now we shall ride rough-shod through Carlton house!' was the immortal vociferation after Percival had fallen. But, it seems, asses have ears as well as hoofs. I could never learn, to a certainty, which of the two noble lords stood listening at the keyhole, while the other was closetted with the king. I only know, that the odium lies between Gr. and Gr.

And husband jests, in hopes, again M. P.
To make one night record seven years of glee.

AUTHOR.

May that night come! Cool C-STL—GH would hear
Polite, his manufactur'd mirth, and cheer;
While the old jolly man, with lighted eye,
And blossom'd face, and wit three bottles high,
Grotesqu'd the congress,—how they carv'd our ball—
How Turkey only was not carv'd at all.—
How Elba's Emperor, one morning fine,
Rode round his kingdom and return'd to dine—
How farmers want for bread by having flour—
How the war cost six thousand pounds an hour.—

And husband jests.]—Mr. Pitt said of SH-R—N, that 'he drew on his memory for wit, and on his imagination for argument.' However, I wish this interesting old stager back again with all my heart. His facetious philippics would, at least, answer as a relief to the supernatural anger and ferocious admonitions of the rest.

How the war cost six thousand pounds an hour.]—I believe this calculation is rather under than over, at least for the last year. But let us trace the statement farther. Six thousands pounds per hour is a hundred pounds per minute, and about a guinea and a half per second. What a freezing piece of arithmetic for B-RD-TT to frighten a mob with! I wonder too, Sir J—N N-WP—T never brought in a bill for the reduction of two pounds per minute in the war expenditure; or the Marquis of L—D—NE, a budget of ways and means to meet the exigencies of the ensuing 31,556,940 seconds. It would be so new and pretty!

Else would he ransack peace for bitter fun,
And merrily shew England quite undone.
  Yes, I contend, this son of Irish bog,
This honest, boozy, red, sublime, droll dog,
Is worth whole hurdles, carted thro' highways,
Of death-faced Br—ms and imprecating Gr–ys.

FRIEND.

Yet T—rn-y sure—

AUTHOR.

Still raises nightly riot,
In the vain hope of being tickled quiet.
Minds, by collision, smoother grow, like wood;
His coarser, as collision curls a flood.
Small taste he entertains for A B C;
And tho' he tries financial one, two, three,
His jabber'd fractions plausibly perplex,
And still, *Inoculus inter cœcos Rex.*

T—rn-y.]—How this patriotic person has fallen! Alas, for those proud days, when he was the idol of dirty Southwark, and when its merchants christened their children after him, in adoration. Soon came the time, however, when its butchers called their dogs by his name, in contempt. Even the house, with all his pasquinading algebra, now look upon him merely as a gay debater. He makes no impression, because they do not consider him in earnest. And yet he is a trifler from sheer desperation. Were the man easier in his mind, I am convinced he would improve.

Inoculus inter cœcos rex.]—I verily believe, if his party could come into power, they would make him Chancellor

Quite unoriginal himself, he scans
Obtuse, all others' œconomic plans.
Aspires to budgets, but accounts ca:ı cast,
So best would serve th' exchequer, station'd last.
Thus 0 proves useless as a leading figure;
The farther back 'tis plac'd, the sum grows bigger.
This pat comparison, from cyphers prest,
Perchance may charm his algebraic breast.
Prompt for the winning as the losing side,
To join like isthmus, or like streight divide;
Official twice, no noise would T—RN-Y make.
The rushing river rested in a lake.
Now place him 'mongst our ministerial men,
My life on't, he grows well behav'd again.
What changes cannot change of place afford!
Legs in the field are wings upon the board.
What in the jug we merely milk esteem,
When pour'd into the ewer, is London cream.

FRIEND.

Great GR-NV-LLE——

AUTHOR.

Let him still dilute his style,
And beat out half a guinea half a mile;

---

of the Exchequer to-morrow! And yet, it is certain, he disappointed his friends sadly when they were in power before. But what can they do? They have not a financial man amongst them.

None heed him. Erewhile, lectur'd on the state,
By PITT in secret, he was counted great.
At length the tyro, scorning to be school'd,
Himself set up, but found his rod o'errul'd;
So soon forsook the more sagacious band,
For those his powers were suited to command.
Inferior by his change of party shewn,
As planets are from stars by motion known.
Now let him curse that warp ambition gave,
And play the fool for those who play the knave;
High with no hopes, important to no ends,
The friend of outcasts, outcast even of friends.

FRIEND.

Yet ER—NE, own, might ELL—B—GH school.

AUTHOR.

And CL-FF—D ER—NE, by the self-same rule.
Paine's advocate, false prophet on the war,

False prophet on the war.]—Government had disappointed his Lordship, so he wrote a pamphlet to prove that grass would grow in the streets of London. But he knows himself that not even brooms thrive there. A barber too had disappointed him; so he wrote a poem predicting cropped heads and unpowdered hair. This prophecy was awfully fulfilled. His Lordship, therefore, has much more to boast as a fop than as a politician. It was on the strength of his pamphlet, I presume, that he too visited the First Consul. His reception was curious. He made his bow: Napoleon asked him if he spoke French; and

Projector of a *nucleus* in a *cor;*
Quaint quibbles shew'd our punning judge profound,
And his wig jingled with the single sound.

FRIEND.

Well, A+B—X+Y L—NDS—NE merits praise.

AUTHOR.

Peace to his dancing and financing days.

---

then, turning round, took snuff. His Lordship, I suppose, took umbrage.

Projector of a nucleus in a cor.]—During the Spanish war, his Lordship used to talk about the expediency of a *nucleus* in the heart of Spain. Many respectable men suspected that he meant a concentration of our forces there. However, all agreed that he meant something or other.

Our punning judge.]—Why may not a judge pun, as well as a bishop? The following is an extract from a sermon in the reign of James the First.

'Here have I *undertaken* one who hath *overtaken* many. A *Machiavellian*, or rather a *matchless villain*. One that professeth himself to be a *friend*, when he is, indeed, a *fiend*.'

A+B—X+Y, L-NDS--NE.]—The first act of the talented administration was to tell the country that its resources were drained almost dry. The next act was to double the Property Tax! Then came the Marquis with a magical budget of virtue to carry on the war for ever and ever, without any additional taxation. John Bull jumped with joy. Man-milliners and pig iron were happy. But, alas, it was soon recollected that M. Dumont (who afterwards assisted Mirabeau in dethroning Louis) had educated the Marquis; and it was suspected that he had also taught his pupil the

Pumps and a budget rais'd him to the skies:
There, pilloried in a cloud, he kicks and cries.

FRIEND.

Yet B-RD-TT holds his station, ne'er to fail—

AUTHOR.

At the mob's head and at the senate's tail.
From daily prints his knowledge is compil'd:
He tosses Magna Charta to his child.
Not quite so low as Blackstone yet descends,
But has great P-RRY at his fingers' ends.

---

financial system of his countryman Neckar. So as this system had already ruined France, plain men began to conjecture that it might likewise ruin England. To conjecture, I say, because nobody (no, not even the Marquis himself) could make head or tail of it. Some thought it was the sinking fund reversed; but all allowed that it resembled nothing so much as Darwin's scheme to replenish human arteries, by transfusing into them, with a syringe, the blood of a calf. His Lordship has never held up his head since.

He tosses Magna Charta to his child.]—A most interesting and most unpremeditated scene was presented to the police, when they broke into Sir FR-N--S's house, on the memorable occasion of his commitment. They found his dear little boy by his side, reading Magna Charta! O pencil of Wilkie! what inferior canvas was then detaining you?

Great P-RRY.]—Editor of the Morning Chronicle. Sir FR-N--S perpetually quotes this print in the House. He likewise picks up much of his information from a person, who eats his hebdomadal dinner with the whisperer of the man, who whispers to the whisperer of Fouche.

Much pains and many thousands he bestows,
To go, where yet he boasts he never goes.
True sportsmen eat not of the game they hit;
He cringes for a seat, but scorns to sit.
And, like some bully, implicates his name,
With what he calls a house of evil fame.

FRIEND.

Yes, fill'd with purchasers of boroughs—

AUTHOR.

Hum.
Contested Westminster costs half a plum.

FRIEND.

Nay, to that hated house he sometimes goes—

AUTHOR.

As men eat rankness, while they curl their nose.
There slaps his heart, and would for England die.
Like Agamemnon, let him slap his thigh.

FRIEND.

Yet jails he visits, and the culprit cheers—

AUTHOR.

Like D'Herbois, patronizes mutineers.

Contested Westminster costs half a plum.]—Considering that Sir Fr-n--s talks so much about the purity of election, odd doings enough took place at Westminster, when he stood candidate. Mills were divided into shares, in order to qualify votes for him; and several wretches, who swore they had votes, were transported for perjury.

Yet jails he visits.]—The Duke of Portland was absolutely obliged, by a circular letter, to prohibit the admission

FRIEND.

Is kind, humane, and loves old England well,
He and his prompters——

AUTHOR.

Pleasant what you tell.
For, of all dangerous men cabal can boast,
A rich fool, led by villains, is the most.

FRIEND.

Let C–RT—GHT, that poor dear old harmless man,
Go preaching on reform, where'er he can.
Who would hamstring his hobby?

AUTHOR.

Ask those hounds,
Who seiz'd him upon most suspicious grounds.

---

of Sir FR-NC-S into any jail whatever throughout the kingdom:—that is, as a visitor; for he afterwards received admission into the Tower as a culprit.

Like D'Herbois, patronizes mutineers.]—Collot D'Herbois first became notorious by pleading the cause of deserters and renegadoes. I trust the parallel between the two men will never extend any farther.

Is kind, humane.]—A man must, I confess, be kind and humane, who has useless old friends, useless old horses, and useless old cows; none of which animals he will either cast off, shoot, or sell. Nevertheless, several of Sir FR-NC-S's friends were hanged in spite of him: others were sent to Botany Bay; two were tried for high treason; one got a thousand lashes, and another cut his throat.

☞ It may not be generally known that the anagram of Sir FR-NC-S B-RD-TT is FRANTIC DISTURBERS.

Who seized him upon most suspicious grounds.]—A bout

FRIEND.

This field is finish'd. Pause. Our cattle smoke.
Another field we plough and then unyoke.

---

three years ago the people of Huddersfield seized this itinerant reformist as a suspicious character. What a pity one is not suffered to make a fuss in peace and quietness!

END OF DIALOGUE THE SECOND.

DIALOGUE THE THIRD.

AUTHOR.

Blest be that nuptial hour, when Charlotte gave
Her hand august to Cobourg good and brave.
Fain would my pen the graceful theme prolong,
But ill suit blossoms with this thorny song.
May she, whom all the letter'd arts endow,
Calm Contemplation thron'd upon her brow,
Receive my future verse. Too happy doom,
If her blue glances shall the page illume.
If lips whose mandates empires will obey,
Pleas'd shall submit their movement to my lay.
For I (if life remain) will England sing,
From her first founder to her latest king.
Her seven compacted crowns, her roses twin'd,
The thistle, shamrock, rose, at last combin'd.
Her sylvan Druids at the mystic stone,
Braint, Derwydd, Ovydd, Awenyddion.
Her victor oak, that dwells upon the waves,
And thunders death thro' all his armed caves,

Braint, Derwydd, Ovydd, Awenyddion.]—The four orders of druids.

Her hero, Wellington, whom Britons call
Another Henry to twice-conquer'd Gaul;
And Nelson, falling where he won the day,
As moons descend amid the main they sway.
So may those holy times when battles cease,
Read how we warr'd for their millenian peace;
Read, till thy name, O Charlotte, mounts in fires,
When the last trumpet sounds and verse expires.

FRIEND.

Well, if old talents with contempt you view,
Confess, at least, the genius of the new.

AUTHOR.

I grant, if merit from reserve we guess,
That none own more, for none exhibit less.
But come, their names.

FRIEND.

High H-LL-D marches first—

AUTHOR.

Like pioneer, the foremost and the worst.
Neat without genius, polish'd without force;
A racer groom'd too slimly for the course;
Let H-LL-D, like a cast of plaster, claim,
From ancestral antiques his mimic fame;

H-LL-ND.]—His Lordship, *like the Prince of Madagascar*, in GLENARVON, loves a quiet life; though he may think it expedient to make a speech, or enter a protest now and then, by way of keeping up a good old family custom.

Draw buried talent to his living head,
And suck, like vampires, fatness from the dead.
Weak, he convenes a council for his guide,
Where M-ck-nt-sh and T-rn-y both preside.
Does what they bid him, (that is understood,)
Nor knows from Adam if 'tis bad or good.
They lacquey his perpetual heels, as Q
Is always followed by obsequious U.
  A borrower from a borrower too is he,
For M-ck-nt-sh from all men borrows free.
In dressing scraps much cookery he shews,
And stitches woodcocks' heads on roasted crows.
All parties he could court, from all withdraw;
Wrote for the lawless, lectur'd on the law.
Recorder, records slighted, took his tone
From metaphysic law beyond our own.
Was doctor, barrister, reviewer, member,
Pittite in June and Foxite in December.
Prais'd Godwin, prais'd king-killers, prais'd the king,
Prais'd bridges as he pass'd, prais'd ev'ry thing.
Then took a taste for anger, and diffus'd
Much pamphlet, and abus'd, abus'd, abus'd.

Wrote for the lawless.]—A notorious pamphlet, called '*Vindiciæ Gallicæ*, or a Defence of the French Revolution and its English Admirers.' This was to please Fox.

Lectur'd on the law.]—In the hall of Lincoln's Inn. This was to please Pitt. He then accepted a place. This was to please himself.

Come B-ks, I pray, look cheery, bristle up;
Try whistling, shake yourself, indulge a sup;
Laugh and be mortal! any thing but bray,
Between two bundles of unchosen hay.
Trust me, 'tis kindness none as kindness quote,
To talk one way and then another vote.
Trust me, extreme distinctions injure right;
White mixt with black is but black mixt with white.
A proneness more to prose than to decide,
Nor heaven, nor earth, nor parliaments abide;
And 'tis with mother state as mother church,
Half helping is quite leaving in the lurch.

FRIEND.

Come, P-NS-NBY, methinks, may well defy
All satire.

AUTHOR.

None commend him more than I.
Kind is his heart, well-principled, humane;
A rock of uncrackt crystal is his brain;
But when rough Whitbread first disturb'd the house,
His rival grew a bear, who was a mouse.
Both to be leaders struggled, Whitbread won
The prize, and genius was by lungs outdone.
Now wherefore sits he, miserably mute,
Head sunk, and boot across unpolish'd boot?

Now wherefore sits he miserably mute.]—At times, indeed, Mr. P-NS--BY gives the house a sudden gust that

Oh, as you hope for fox-chase or renown,
Talk Br–m, that unapprov'd pretender, down!

FRIEND.

No, Br–m, as leader, patriots more admire;
Like Whitbread in discretion, wit and fire.

---

threatens its very hinges. Nobody can guess why. Some will have it, that he now wants to out-Br—m Br—m, as he once wanted to out-Whitbread Whitbread. Be this as it may, his manners are quite altered. Formerly he spoke much and mildly. Now he speaks little and petulantly. He should consult decorum. At all events, he should wear clean boots.

No, Br—m, as leader, patriots more admire.]—Every one knows that Mr. Br—m is thrusting himself forward as the successor of Whitbread. One laughs to see the man struggling into consequence, affecting a high tone, and tremendously protesting that he will probe some bagatelle or other to the inmost quick. No man of four thousand a-year, and Br—m's friend, can hope to remain in peaceable possession of his property, without Br—m's informing the house that he has a friend of four thousand a-year. No acquaintance of note in the house can hope to be called otherwise by him, than his honorable friend. His honorable friend, however, generally returns the compliment by calling him the learned gentleman. Lastly, no adjective, even of the most awful signification, can hope to pass his mouth, without being coupled with the word *pretty*. Things are pretty terrible, pretty odious, pretty disgusting, and pretty formidable—expressions, in my opinion, *pretty ugly*.

AUTHOR.

So songs we call like music of the sphere,
Which never gentleman contriv'd to hear.
So Milton could his Eve far lovelier call,
Than several persons who ne'er liv'd at all.
Hard-headed demagogue! by hacknies hackt,
Expos'd misstater of notorious fact;
Grand spokesman-general for three silent tongues,
BR—M is a thorough whig, heart, head and lungs.

So Milton could his Eve far lovelier call, than several persons who ne'er liv'd at all.]—

———'More lovely fair,
Than woodnymph, or the fairest goddess *feign'd*,
Of three that in Mount Ida naked strove.' *Par. Lost.*

This may certainly be termed a blunder. Johnson has remarked others in Milton; such as, 'What *stood, recoiled.*' Yet Johnson himself is not without one. He gave this line to Goldsmith,

'To *stop* too fearful and too faint to *go*.'

If the man could neither stand still, nor move forward, he must, I think, have spun round in one spot. Thus too, Gray says,

'T' alarm th' *eternal midnight* of the grave.'

Surely what has not an end, cannot have a middle. Pope also says,

'And *sleepless* lovers, just at twelve, *awake*.'

Grand spokesman-general for three silent tongues.]—Mr. BR—M, it is said, boasts that he has a voting party of

What would content him?—He deserts the bar,
To try the house—would peerage, would a star?
Fly, fly; bestar his heart, nor then forget
To strew bleak ocean with the violet!

FRIEND.

Yes, when skies vanish, and this earthly ball,
When broken suns in faded splinters fall;
When other worlds and other skies succeed,
Then might his rosy mouth demand a meed;
And just one cluster of the zodiac claim,
To write in stars his Caledonian name!
But for such stars as Rundell makes—

AUTHOR.

Yet hear:
Try, only try—three hundred pounds a year.
Now casting in dead rats and loathsome things,
He makes his mouth a puddled ditch for kings.
Bourbons and Brunswicks in the scum are stirr'd—
Indeed the Stuarts get a kinder word.

'three silent tongues.' I doubt whether he can command even one tongue. Certainly not his own.

Indeed the Stuarts get a kinder word.]—The whole annals of Parliament cannot furnish so shameful and indecent an attack upon royalty as this ultra-patriot lately made in the house. He had not even the fine ingenuous rashness of youth to plead. No; his was the cold, sallow, grinning premeditation of a Scotch hypercritic. His own party shrank from the tirade in horror; and about twenty

By him mean trifles are tremendous made;
A smuggler moves him more than stagnant trade.
Large seeds of lupin, thus, small growth are given,
While tiny mustard sends its tree to heaven.
Thus this Anteater hunts not game that leaps,
But lolls his slimy tongue to catch what creeps.
The moment BR--M pronounces, 'something wrong,'
'Hear!' shouts each Ex, the lobbies 'hear!' prolong.
Chophouses clamour, newspapers indite,
And 'something wrong' soon turns to 'nothing right.'
Pil'd Babels of petitions heaven ascend,
And call Reform from Hebrid to Land's-end.
Thus when old Afric kings a sneeze began,
Thro' courtiers round an acclamation ran.
With courtiers round, the servants yell'd outside;
The whole house, women, children, dogs reply'd.
The people in the streets took up the shout,
The people bawl'd who were not walking out.
Till city, country, cottage, castle, farm,
Road, village, hamlet, rang with one alarm.

---

of the more moderate amongst them went over, on that question, to the ministers. He recanted afterwards, I must confess; but the pitiful flourish came too late. It was the frightened snail defending itself with its froth, after it had sheathed its horns and shrunk into its shell.

Old Afric kings.]—The kings of Monomotapa.

So that whene'er an Afric monarch sneez'd,
One long-resounding roar his spacious empire seiz'd!

FRIEND.

To him and H-RN-R some excuse is due;
Both scribblers in an unreserv'd review.

H-RN-R.]—This gentleman, on the whole, is one of the most respectable aspirants to the honor of teasing ministers. But he has no talents for a real thorough-going downright demagogue. Besides, plaintive indignation, laborious eloquence, looks of gloom and tones of peevishness, will never recommend his learning. A skull would make rather a forbidding flower-pot. The Speculative Club, too, has spoiled Mr. H-RN-R, even though Dugald Stewart educated him.

Both scribblers in an unreserved review.]—I am informed that the Editor of the Edinburgh Review is really rather a rational man in politics, but that the writers whom he employs sometimes turn out, like other journeymen, and refuse to work any longer, unless he will insert their jacobinical effusions without remorse. One can almost forgive Englishmen who write like Scotch Reviewers, but there is no pardon for Scotch Reviewers who write like Frenchmen.

As to the mere language of the work, it is no more English than the sentiments. Whoever wishes to read sentences with eight or nine contiguous 'fors, withs, and tos,'—three or four enfeebling 'would have beens,' and 'might have beens,'—nominative cases made ablatives absolute,—'him being' instead of 'his being,'—'thereafter,' 'eminentest,' 'mighty little,' and 'standing up for a thing,'—may find all these blossoms of speech, (as I have just now found them) in a ten minutes' survey of the Edinburgh Review.

How could two men, forgetting gainful ire,
Have tongues of water, who have pens of fire?

AUTHOR.

Yet artful H-RN-R can his tongue command.
His motives some respect, some understand.
No cool rebuff from his disgusted prince,
Makes him a flaming patriot ever since.
Alike unskill'd to flatter or inflame,
His aspect, accent, action still the same,
He shuns adorning arts, and seems to think,
Beer, in dull pewter, tastes a better drink.
With that wise seeming men for wisdom take;
With projects which can neither mar nor make;
He to no fierce anathema gives scope,
Far more of the Pretender than the Pope.

Whoever desires to see opposite opinions upon politics and poetry, supported in the same work, may consult the Edinburgh Review.

Whoever has a fancy for Teutonic, unvowelled, unpronounceable names, will find plenty of Trojanisches Kreig, Chrimhildren Rache, Kijric, Stumpfe-Reime, Klingende-Schal-Reime, Strong Bopp and Martin Gumpel, pedantically at his service in the Edinburgh Review.

Whoever hopes to have Louis Capet nick-named (as the Sans Culottes nick-named his brother) Louy Cappy, may hereafter, perhaps, see his wishes realized in the Edinburgh Review.

FRIEND.

Yet W-NN, Sir, Cambrian W-NN, has no pretence—

AUTHOR.

To what? to Speaker, or to common sense?
Each night, the big man's little lungs respire,
Retrench, reform, displace, disband, retire.
So the Welsh Carollers a patois din,
When bolted out, in hope of getting in.
How squeaks his octave fife to W-TK-NS' drum!
Strange, from his giantship such shrieks should come.
Just as thro' some huge chimney, high up-pil'd,
'Sweep!' cries the screaming treble of a child.

To what? To Speaker?]—People laugh at this man of precedents for aspiring to be speaker; but I think without good ground; for the speaker (by the figure *lucus a non lucendo*) speaks less than any member in the house.

How squeaks his octave fife to W-TK-NS' drum.]—The piping sharpness of Mr. W--NN's voice is so oddly contrasted with the guttural rumbling of his brother's, that both gentlemen are called by the members, 'bubble and squeak.' Fatal nick-name!—bubble and squeak. By Castor and Pollux, 'tis too bad. What would ancestor Kadrod say to this? What would the great Madox ap Gruffyd Maelor say to this? How the shade of Caractacus would shudder on the Welsh hills, if,

Bubble and squeak, the woods,
Bubble and squeak, the floods,
Bubble and squeak, the rocks and hollow mountains rung!

FRIEND.

His tiny voice would prove his soul profound.
An empty barrel makes a thund'ring sound.

AUTHOR.

Yet not by shrillness patriotism we know,
'Sweep,' cry'd above, shews fire extinct below.

FRIEND.

Come, what of F-LK-NE?

AUTHOR.

Oh! his first advance,
To wretched notice, came by curious chance.
A question, quite unseconded, was mov'd;
He seconded, ('tis fact!) ere he approv'd.
Sweet candor! hence his patriotism began,
Hence he gained audience of a courtezan.
Hence an upholsterer patroniz'd the youth;
Hence W-RDLE, C-BB-T, and the ghost of Truth.
Gay in the boudoir, in the senate grim,
He cozen'd CL-RKE, and then CL-RKE jilted him.

F--LK--NE.]—If this accidental—accidental patriot would speak with—with a little less hesi—hesitation, he might become a patriot of much mischievous—much mischievous garrulity. But the devil—devil of it, is, that the good of his country always sticks—sticks—sticks in his—his throat —always sticks in his throat!

C-BB--T.]—Poor BILLY C-BB--T! his Register has just arrived at a state of stagnation. Let the puddle grow putrid in peace. I shall not disturb its odours.

Lord of Augean jobs, in F-LK-NE see,
How nicety and nastiness agree.
Yet 'tis by stooping men ascend a steep;
We climb in the same attitude we creep.

FRIEND.

There is one B-NN-T—what is B-NN-T, tell?

AUTHOR.

Remarkable for squabbling in Pall-Mall.
Because a soldier jib'd him somewhat tart,
Six hundred senators must take his part.
Because a redcoat flourish'd with his sword,
Our army must disband, upon my word!
For B-NN-T and the turkeycock wax wroth,
And fluster at a scrap of scarlet cloth.
Poor man! beneath his microscopic scope,
An eyelash of a lady seems a rope.
A civil gentleman at home, they say;
But special thund'ring is his public way.

Remarkable for squabbling in Pall-Mall.]—Whenever a patriot cannot get on in Pall-Mall, he is sure to get on at St. Stephens's. I think I hear this *careering* gentleman, as he wheels round his horses from the fray, cry out with an assuring slap on the knee, 'My Lord, if we don't make a good thing of this, I'll be shot!' Yet he did not make quite so good a thing of the sinecure question. There he went inhumanly careering against his own family.

FRIEND.

That Neckar from Geneva, learned Sir Sam,
Who long'd to say 'your ladyship,' not 'ma'am,'
He well deserves applause.

AUTHOR.

Applause he wins,
For ending cool, tho' spiteful he begins;
And angry by anticipation, takes
Offence, before one soul an answer makes.
This restless Solon would so alter law,
Even our Great Charter trembles for a flaw.
Point upon point he heaps, and looking round,
Feels himself posed, so thinks himself profound.
A lawyer, if unpaid, is mute as mouse:
A statesman, if unpaid, will stun the house.
Reverse may hold.—Give R-M-LLY a fee,
He proses forth—a place, how dumb were he!
Bid him the senate for the bar forsake;
Bad wine, we know, good vinegar may make.

That Neckar from Geneva.]—Sir Samuel's family were originally Genevese. Neckar was a Genevese. Rousseau was a Genevese. Dumont, LORD L—ND—NE's tutor, was a Genevese. Voltaire lived at Geneva. Gibbon lived at Geneva. What the plague have mankind done to Geneva, that she should use them so?

FRIEND.

Last let me mention M-TH-N——what of him?

AUTHOR.

A Tory when content, a Whig by whim.
A well-drest patriot, willing to devote
His time between his country and his coat.
If statesmen raise his choler, tailors, you,
(This pun for ER-NE,) raise his collar too.

FRIEND.

The man means well.

AUTHOR.

Means nothing, good or bad;
A politic impolitic mere lad.
At six, he ponders on what superfine
His beauship shall adopt—what vote, at nine.
One question or one button out of place,
'Gainst Minister and Snip he sets his face.
Pass those who sit hereditary fools,
By right armorial of bar, or and gules;

A Tory when content, a Whig by whim.]—Mr. M-TH-N apostasized so abruptly, that he fears to be temperate lest it should be doubted that he is sincere. The old Talents are happy to lay hold of him. Indeed, they pick up with avidity any man who has not yet lost his good name. They keep Messrs. H-RN-R, B-NN-T, W-NN, and M-TH-N, as a sort of reserved corps, yet unfleshed in degradation, and ready to march forward on the last emergency of character.

Those who their fame to charnell'd ashes trust,
As diamonds owe their polish but to dust.

Ye rosy Burghers, whose fat lids o'erdroop
With former turtle and transmuted soup;
Let slim Westenders of starvation talk;
The world wags well with those who cannot walk.
No hang'd forefathers make ye Brunswick's haters,
No grandsons ye of sons of sons of traitors;
Boast ledgers all, not genealogic books,
Proud to be patriotic pastrycooks.
What is best blood? methinks the richest fed.
Old families and rose-trees lose their red.
How BR-M would warm, if venison were his food,
Who even on oatmeal can so chafe his blood!
A tortoise props the globe, as some relate;
By dint of turtle, W—D may save the state.

By dint of turtle, W—D may save the State.]—The bust of Buonaparte——shall I spare him? In good sooth I will. The poor man knew no more about the bust, than Mr. H-BH--SE knows about the original. That is a nice young gentleman. Upon my word, his letters from France do him infinite honor. His beginning to cry because Napoleon read a petition, was in the first style of sensibility; and when Napoleon ran away, nothing could exceed the sweet waspishness of his infantine upbraidings. Dids 'em vex my child? Dids 'em take its nown nown Nemperor away from it? Hushaden, hushaden!

That W-TH-N loves his country, clear I hold;
Viragoes love poor devils who let them scold.
Nor can Q—N hate those ministerial sinners,
Who move his wrath to eat abusive dinners.
Even G-DB-RE, when frank with public wine,
Must own that angry men right merry dine.

Such are our precious Talents, old and new,
Who now for power, (sole object they pursue,)
Make their last effort, ere those troubles cease,
Which, well they know, must ever follow Péace.
All their stock-pieces of performance spent,
Sad dogs! what now remains for discontent?

W-TH--N.]—I remark that people of much labelled linen and critical acumen, are apt to treat public men as they do grammar, by making the second person more worthy than the first.

This sentence being somewhat abstruse, I ought to have translated it into bad English, for the benefit of Mr. W--TH--N. Whoever presided over the grammatical department of his pamphlet upon eating, left several little slips in the first six pages. I could never read farther.

Must own that angry men right merry dine.]—If I asked the worthy Alderman whether he would *accede* to this opinion, he might say, 'Yes;' but if I asked him, whether he would *subscribe* to it, he would shake his negativing head, and say, '*Certainly not.*'

FRIEND.

Nay, still O'C-NN-LL and some twenty more,
Vex Ireland with much Catholic uproar.

AUTHOR.

But good Fingal still waves his calming hand,
In all the awful grace of meek command.
Serene, yet firm, his wisdom knows to make,
Foes by design, act allies by mistake.
More converts to the cause his worth has won,
Even in one year, than ages else had done.

Ireland.]—It is now the fashion to say, that Ireland is beggared, because she cannot pay the demands made upon her, and because her bankruptcies are so numerous. No supposition can be more false. Her trade (and therefore her capital) is increasing yearly. The value of her exports was,

In 1809................£5,739,843.
In 1814................ 7,139,437.

The vast increase of her imports, both in raw materials for the industrious, and in articles of luxury for the opulent, also proves her increasing prosperity. Since the union, her imports of woollen and cotton cloths have doubled; of carpets, silks, glasses, &c., tripled. Her imports of wine have doubled; those of blankets have increased as ten to one; and likewise those of musical instruments and jewellery. Her present distresses, like England's, have arisen from an impeded circulation, in consequence of excessive, though inevitable loans; and no doubt the effect will cease with the cause.

Fierce zealots, vext that virtue makes him great,
Hate him for not affording cause of hate;
And factions, wanting sense to praise him, claim
At least the sense of fearing to defame.

FRIEND.

Yet mark, at home, what lowering skies appear!
Third secretaries threat, and poison'd beer.
What tho' all France before our spirit fell?
One saucy guardsman lords it in Pall-Mall.

Neither are we to calculate her deterioration by the number of her bankruptcies. In 1700, when the failures in England were but thirty-eight, the exports amounted but to £6,045,432. In 1793, when the bankruptcies were 1304, the exports amounted to £20,390,180. In that year of terror, the nation was informed, as usual, how nothing could save her. And yet in 1814 (twenty-three years after), her exports amounted to £56,591,514!

Catholic uproar.]—Almost all the Catholic aristocracy have seceded from the turbulent part; who, though they call the loudest for emancipation, are, in reality, the least desirous of it: because they rose into notice on its shoulders, and must sink into insignificance at its termination. But Englishmen, in general, from their personal ignorance of the Sister Island, have an idea that all Catholics are hostile to the Constitution. I wish such men, instead of going over to Waterloo, and bringing back sanguinary keepsakes, would visit Ireland, and import a little knowledge of the Irish people. The fact is, whenever an Englishman does perform the exploit of a trip to the Emerald Isle, he finds himself treated with peculiar respect and

What tho' we millions upon millions save?
Ten salaries may send England to her grave.
Besides, there's this and that, and that and this;
And sly Napoleon—hark—'twere not amiss.
Still may himself, or his imperial race,
Unhinge creation from the hooks of space.

AUTHOR.

He falls, he falls! Oh, never more restored,
The gnashing tyrant bites his broken sword.
Th' infernal game of glorious murder lost,
A victory at cards is now his boast.

Then welcome, panting and twice-mission'd dove!
Black rains no more are rushing from above:
The deluge shrinks, and gradual to the skies,
The desolate and streaming mountains rise;

---

hospitality. He begins to regret having insured his life, and he ventures to unload his pistols. If he does not eat more pudding, at least he laughs at more wit than he ever did before, and even learns to laugh in the right place. Nay, he undertakes to grow witty himself, and his efforts are treated with polite encouragement. In short, finding himself much courted and quite lively, the good gentleman begins to fancy the place a paradise; and at length, when his business is concluded (for all this time he never neglected his business), he returns reluctantly home to the bosom of his family, who stare in astonishment, not unmixed with terror, at the sprightliness of his deportment, and the unintelligibility of his puns.

And woody spots above the flood are seen,
Points of white rocks and uplands shining green.

FRIEND.

Mourn then ye Whigs, your fallen Napoleon mourn.
Involv'd in his disaster, sigh forlorn.
Had that great villain thriven, ye trusted well,
Cross England soon would Ministers expel.
Now, sad reverse, your hopes together fall,
And one vile Waterloo has crusht you all!
Down fall poor Lucien, Er—ne, Bertrand, Gr-y,
Murat and L-nd-ne, P-ns-by and Ney;

One word at parting, to my friends the talents. Though I know they consider error their hereditary right, and an attempt to deprive them of it a conspiracy to rob them of their property, I should hope they would at last perpetrate one act of candor, and confess the full and perfect failure of all their evil omens, for five-and-twenty years. They prophesied that 'the glorious fabric of human wisdom,' the French Revolution, would produce nothing but happiness. It has brought unmixed misery. They prophesied that the war in Spain would ruin us. It has saved us. They prophesied that Buonaparte would conquer the World. The World has conquered him. They prophesied that they would make peace with him. He would not make peace with them. They prophesied that the resources of France would outlast our own. Our own have outlasted those of France.

So much for the past. Now for the future. They feel

With Jerome, GR-N-LLE is in equal plight,
And drunken Joe and Dick are ousted quite;
While vainly, for the Scotch and Corsic throne,
Small Nappy cuts his teeth, B——M shews his own.

AUTHOR.

Yes, had such factious Gauls and Britons stood,
Unwarped supporters of the public good;
Those, not afflicting earth with crimes and evils,
These, not bepraising the dark deeds of devils;
Even Carnot now might hold the seals of France;
Even T-RN-Y some small desk in our finance;
And 'All the Talents,' at this moment mad,
Might still retain the little wits they had.

---

infinitely angry that armies are kept in France, to prevent her from commencing another revolution, and devastating Europe once more. After the most grotesque and dreadful experiments upon liberty—after those anarchical incantations, which had conjured up a thousand limping apparitions of impossible perfection—after a series of monthly constitutions, where at first all were rulers, then five, then three, and at last one; and where each agreed with the other, in nothing but the principle of universal devastation, the monster now lies bound beneath our feet, and yet our patriots would fain let it loose upon mankind again! At least, it is consistent, that men who began with upholding the French Revolution, should end with recommending measures which favor its revival. Yet nothing but their adherence to this jacobinical principle, and to those others which arose out of it, has made the British people so pertinacious in

FRIEND.

Enough.—St. James's strikes six dining peals:
Quick clank the flags with horse-shoed human heels;
Gigs in full dust make space atone for time,
And shades of chimnies fronts of houses climb.

AUTHOR.

Cease then; for ample ink my finger stains:
No page unscrawl'd of all my quire remains.

---

rejecting them as a ministry. No wonder, then, the men are enraged to madness. No wonder they mould images of calamity themselves, and then mourn over them with the whine of a termagant, and with two-fisted sensibility. Restriction in their ambitious projects appears to have narrowed even their minds. During their short administration, this truth became evident. They sent out nice little expeditions and fresh-water armaments; made crackers, pored over diplomatic precedents, and requested Talleyrand to accept the assurances of their high consideration; while the world was receding beneath their feet, and the portentous meteors of the times were melting the elements around them. He whose country is his object, feels his powers grow with the greatness of events; as the eagle rises higher in a tempest than in a calm. But nothing can operate an alteration on the man of party. Like the stagnant pool, he never stirs beyond his circumscribed boundary; while the rolling waters of Genius and of Wisdom, purifying, adorning, diffusing life and joy and utility in their progress, still rush for-

Pared to the feather by repeated knives,
My pen, like Opposition, scarce survives.

---

ward towards their predestinated limits, to fulfil the immutable decree.

END.

B. Clarke, Printer, Well Street, London.

Lightning Source UK Ltd.
Milton Keynes UK
UKOW05f1103060716

277733UK00001B/111/P